HOW TO ESCAPE FROM PRISON, WITHOUT LEAVING YOUR CELL

BY

REV. JOSHUA RODRIGUEZ

ISBN 98-1-7367843-2-7 (paper) 2012 first edition; 2021 Second edition

ABOUT THE AUTHOR

Rev. Joshua Rodriguez is an author, public speaker, and successful businessman. He and His wife Evangelist Gayle Rodriguez are the founders of Sons of Light Ministries, World Harvest Church, and World Harvest Ministries. World Harvest Ministries have the vision for worldwide outreach to the unsaved and the incarcerated men and women.

We believe that the time that you will be in prison does not have to be wasted time or a time of deterioration. On the contrary, with some effort on your part and the help of Almighty God, this could be one of the most productive periods of your life.

The principles you will find in this book have their foundation in the Word of God. They are a solid foundation to live the God kind of life that Jesus promised us in His Word (John 10:10) They are applicable to your situation whether you are doing a one-year sentence or a life term.

It was my incredible journey of 15 years and five months through the prison system, and the reality of the Word of God, that inspired me to share this experience and the principles the Lord unveiled to live a productive Christian life while serving prison time.

I was asked to be referred to as Brother Joshua in order to bring all the attention to my Master, and not to himself. He has also purposely left out non-essential information related to the crime that led to my incarceration and the many details of prison life which are not relevant to this teaching. It is my desire that you focus on the message and not the messenger.

The Bible commands us to put our eyes and faith in Jesus who is the author and developer of our faith. This book was created to present you with information that will guide you to Jesus and that will strengthen you to walk in a manner worthy of his calling.

Acknowledgments

I would like to recognize the great contribution of my wife of 25 years, Gayle, for her dedication to typing, and proofreading this manuscript. I am also great full to all my family members who supported me during my incarceration period and the individuals who assisted me in achieving my goal of freedom. There are many ministers, law enforcement agents, correctional officers, and even strangers who were led by God to help me in my pursuits. You know who you are, to you I dedicate this book.

TABLE OF CONTENTS

INTRODUCTION

At the time of this second edition, prison statistics are over the top. The United States has more people incarcerated than any other nation in the world. In 2019 over 2.3 million people were confined in US jails and prisons.

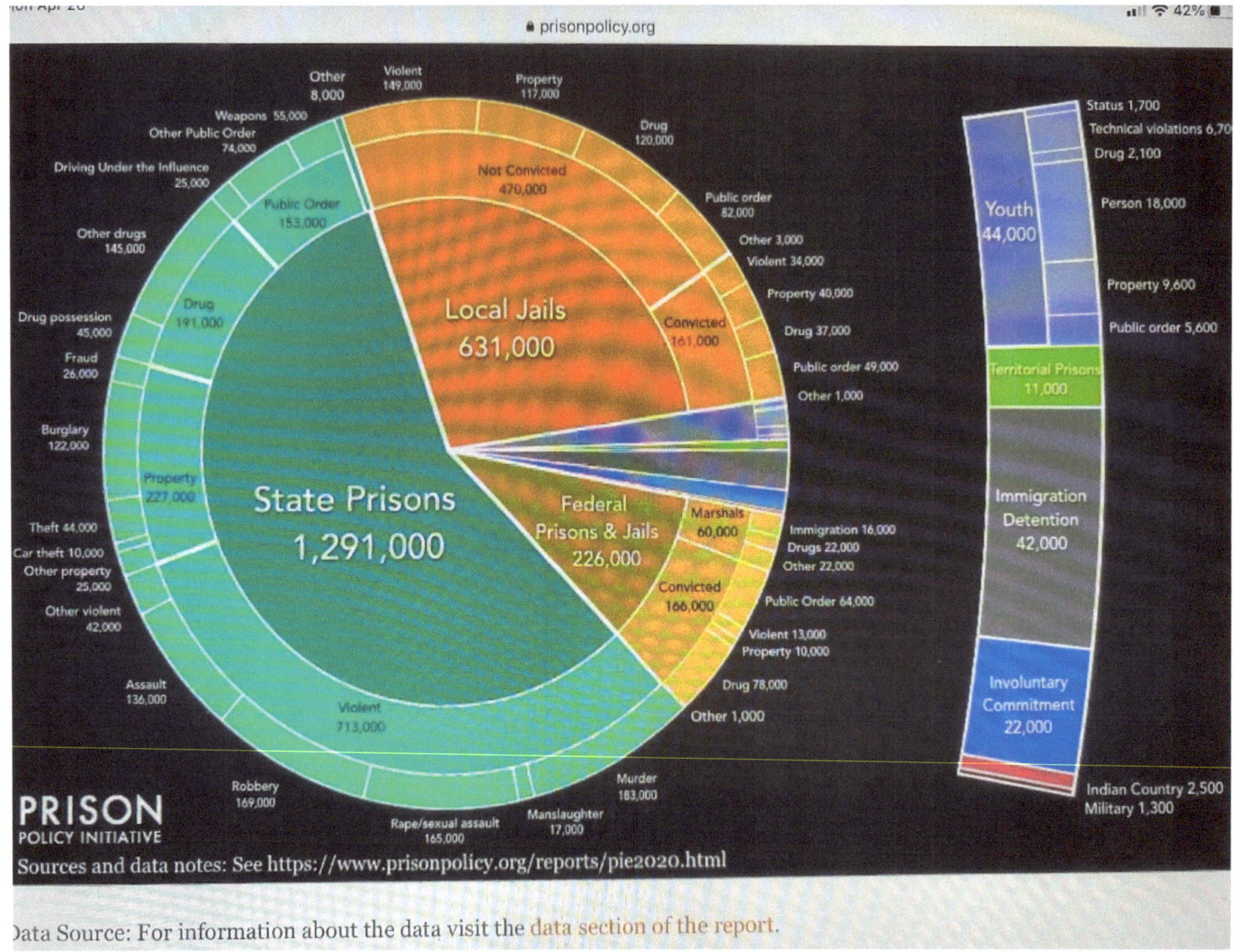

)ata Source: For information about the data visit the data section of the report.

The government does not have any solution to this problem since they are only are targeting the symptom of a sick society.

The only solution to a sick society is to be treated by Dr. Jesus Christ the healer and savior of the world. I was part of the prison system for 15 years and five months. I was set free in order to work for God. And in this spirit, I wrote this book.

"How to escape from prison without leaving your cell", was the first book I wrote after being released from prison in 1999. The original purpose of the book was to reach the growing prison population in the United Estates. So, I decided to write my story and the many lessons I learned while incarcerated for a period of fifteen years and five months (15 yrs. 5 mo.).

However, my 3exerience can be a learning curve for anyone dealing with difficult situations in life. One thing I learned was that there more people in prison out in the communities than those behind bars. And Jesus can set them free as well as those behind bars. For Jesus is the prisoner's best friend.

The second goal in this second edition of my book is to share some spiritual insight to those who have received Jesus as their Lord but have many issues in their Christian walk. See, many people try to tell us that changing from a worldly mindset into the renovated mindset of Christianity is something easy to do, and that we are going to walk on a path of roses having success in everything we do.

But I come to tell you that life is difficult that changes will not happen until you get to a total convinced of their need. See, we are a product of our belief, and what we do is just putting in action what we think is right, Nothing more and nothing less. That why the Bibles tell us "Not to be conforming with this world but be ye transformed by the RENEWING OF YOUR MIND." Rom 12:2-3. The instructions on this book are given for free, but they are not cheap. It has cost me many painful years of seeking, praying, and doing what I have received from the Lord.

As I said in my first edition, I am not writing a book about my prison stories, even though they are fascinating seeing the Lord at work, but I am writing for you to know the main force behind the story, the Lord Jesus.

At the writing of this book, there are more than 2.3 million people incarcerated in the United Estates. At a rate of 698 people per 100,000. There are 1,719 state prisons, 109 federal prisons, 1772 juvenile correction facilities, 3163 local jails, and 80 Indian county jails... (Wikipedia 2019).

Crime in America is shaped by many forces including, upbringing, environmental, economic and social disadvantages. But mainly is the confusion among the people of their moral values and compass. When you don't know who you are, and what are you supposed to be doing in life many forces will invite you to do whatever it takes to get ahead in life, including criminal activities.

In my experience, finding God and using His Word as a compass for my life did the change, I needed. I have been changed by the Word of God, washed in His blood, and place on a road of success. Now, you get to read my story....

CHAPTER ONE

Coming to prison, Is it all over?

Coming to prison is the most dramatic experience any human being could ever experience. It could be compared to the loss of your vital senses or more poetically speaking the strangulation of your soul. The pain and sorrow over the loss of one's freedom have no comparison in the world. Only those who have experienced it know the depth and intensity of the pain caused by imprisonment.

Falling into the black hole of the judicial system is anyone's worse nightmare. Beginning with the arrest, which is usually a dramatic one, and followed by the judicial process of pretrial stages, your life is turned upside down. At this point, our world of power and privacy is destroyed. All the things we have "worked so hard" to achieve are consumed in a moment.

Multiple court proceedings along with outrageous attorney fees leave us discouraged and flat broke. It is during this time that all charges are laid out and the destiny of our lives is handled by lawyers and prosecutors. That process will reach a point in which we are asked to make a choice. The choice is basically what terms you will go to prison, or as they call it, a plea bargain.

At this point in time, the confusion of the moment combined with bad legal advice from a mediocre attorney leads us to a dead-end (whether you are guilty or not the pressure is unbearable). Yes, here is when the attorney may state that he can get you out "for they have nothing against you" That advice will eventually fade away as the prosecutor presents a solid case (even with some surprise witnesses), but this won't happen before our money goes into the lawyer's hand.

Then, the attorney's strategy changes to get you the least possible sentence.

TIME, I DON'T WANT TO DO NO TIME!! I can hear this sentence.

echoing all over the Metropolitan Correction Center N.Y. Well, wake up and smell the coffee; you are going to do time.

Having finished the legal process guaranteed by the U.S. Constitution, and sentenced under the provision of the Minimum Mandatory Sentence (New Law) you are sent to prison to serve the mandated by the guidelines under the minimum mandatory sentence (at least in the federal system).

Contrary to the outcome we expected, we find ourselves on our way to prison. Yes, the transfer "stinks". I was transferred from New York MCC to Lewisburg, Pa in a four-hour drive without access to a bathroom, shackled, and handcuffed with a black box, which cuts off your blood circulation. Later in another transfer, I took the Federal Bureau of Prison Conair with 60 other guys. If you decided you have to use the bathroom during the flight, you will have to work hard to clean yourself. Just as I said before prison transfer stinks!

Hey, if you find yourself reading this book at this stage, do not be discouraged. Your life is not over. This is the time to adjust your thinking to the new reality.... prison. Hey, you can argue with me all day, but that will not change the fact that you are in prison. In order to cope with this new reality, What I began to do was to get in my mind that I had a long journey to go and that my best bet was to concentrate on using that time to give God an opportunity to work in my life. I realized that for the last two decades of my life I had not even thought about the existence of God. I was my own god. I even read and studied man-made theories that denied the existence of God. Ha!!! Think again. I soon learned that I was not a god as I walked through the prison gates.

"From *heaven the Lord viewed the earth, to hear the groaning of the prisoners, to release those appointed to death... Psalm 102:20."*

PRISON VISITATION

Once we enter prison, visitation privilege is the first demand we place on the penal system. This demand is so important that we are not willing to wait for the Correctional Counselor to make our visiting list. Well, I have news for you. It will take a while to have the list approved. We don't care that there are 300 guys waiting for him, we want it now! So, instead of fighting the Counselor, have him approve a special visitor's pass. If you really want the pass, be nice, don't cuss him out. It will not help you in the long run.

Once you're visiting list is ready, you need to prepare for your first visit. Visitation is our most valuable time. This is the time when we can see our families, hug the kids, and give a good kiss to the honey.

A word of caution, go by the rules and don't go any farther. If you mess up you will regret it for the rest of your life. Hey, I got more news for you. There are rules in the visiting room. The truth is the prison authorities can take your visitation rights for almost any reason. Learn to pick your fights!!!! If you insist on breaking the visiting room rules, this is one battle that you most certainly will lose! According to the prison authorities, Visitation is not a right but a privilege. Men, I hated that phrase. I was told that many times, and I argued. But the truth is that prison authorities can take your visitation rights for almost any reason. I know that you may think," I'll show them." But they don't go that route. When you fight for something fights to win.

See, most guys think that they can still beat the system. But the fact is, if you could not beat it outside the fence, what makes you think that you will get away with it in a small, controlled environment?

Let me speak to you frankly. There is something I call the "Visitation syndrome" (the reaction people have toward prisoners). In this syndrome, various groups of people will react differently under the pressure that prison exerts on them. Most likely, there will be three groups of people that will initially come to see you.

The first group of people that will stop coming to see you will be your friends (including girlfriends). They will try to avoid seeing you there for many reasons. In some cases, they think it is too painful. Others feel that it is too risky, while others my think that it is unprofitable. You know the old saying, "The king is dead, long live the (new) king."

The second group that I stop visiting you are your spouse and kids. This usually occurs over a period of time. At first, the visits may be frequent, but then the wife may stop coming but every so often. There are many reasons she will give you. But the result will be the same, no visits. All this process will be accelerated if you come to the Visiting Room with a plan to put pressure on your relatives. If you do this, you will end up discouraging them from coming back to see you.

Then there are our Mothers. Mothers will still come when everybody else has deserted you. They suffer for you and as long as the finances permit, they will keep coming.

Now that I have your attention, whether you are mad at me or in agreement, let me tell you how I overcame this syndrome.

1. Do not demand your friends to come to visit all the time. It is better to commit some of them to send you some money for your needs. Even this won't last too long.

2. When your kids are visiting, dedicated time to them. Don't spend all your time trying to kiss Mommy. Play with them and make the visit a pleasant time. Make them want to come back.

3. Your wife needs to be loved and appreciated more than anything. Contrary to men's beliefs, women need more love and affection than sex. Hey, women are different. When she comes to visit recognize her efforts, make her feel that she is the only one in the world that matters. Ask her to come sometime without the kids so that you can talk more freely. Remember she thinks that you've earned your sentence. Don't blame or demand money or favors. Don't mix her with other inmates' wives. That will not help. Please do not ask her to do anything that might embarrass her in any way in public. Too many times I saw visitations canceled right on the spot because the men got too hot and wanted her to .... shame of them. Treat your wife with respect, love, affection, and she will probably stay with you until the end.

4. The Mothers. Mother is an incredibly special visitor. They are suffering more than anyone else. You are part of her flesh and bones and no matter what you have

done you are still her baby. Deal with Mom in a positive way. Tell her how sorry you are for the bad things you have done and emphasized the productive life you are developing in prison. In particular the spiritual changes and investment you are making. Stop nagging or demanding that she send you money. Remember, she has no financial obligation to you, especially if you did not take care of her when you had plenty of money.

I realize that there is so much advice I could give you pertaining to your conduct in prison, but I will finalize this section by saying that if you conduct yourself like a man who is Christ-like you will gain the respect of the population. If on the contrary, you decided to act like a jerk you will reap what you sowed. Remember the definition of insanity, "doing the same thing, and expecting different results."

MY FIRST YEARS IN PRISON

The most difficult years in prison are the first couple of years. During the first few months, a lengthy process of classification takes place. If your pre-sentence investigation report is not well done you could end up in the wrong place. If the Pre-Sentence Investigation report (PSI) contains wrong information or even allegations from "witnesses" you might end up in a medium or high-level security facility, even when your offense is not very severe. In addition, you will be placed on the "special list" that institutions have for troublemakers. That list will give the institution the names of people who are to be locked down immediately if any disturbance may appear in the facility.

At any rate, this period of time is difficult, but it will end. A crisis is not. going to last forever. Now, you are in a crisis. So, hang in there and don't get an attitude that may jeopardize a good classification. This is the time for you to act responsibly before the authorities and ask God for favor during the classification process. You need to get a good facility close to home.

That will enable you to have regular visits and feel peace of mind. I was transferred from one institution to another until finally, I reached my final destination close to home (New York). Then things began to settle down as I began to study, work, and practice some sports.

CHAPTER TWO

Rationalizing—Why did this happen???

As you become part of this new prison society you will have to deal with both the spiritual and practical areas of your life. Here I place the first for that is what you are: you are a spiritual being who has a (mind, will, and emotions) and you dwell in a physical body.

While settling into prison routine, there is come to be a time to satisfy the mind with answers. You will start to search for the reason or reasons that caused your incarceration. You may begin to think that the reason you are in prison is that someone told on you, or that you could have done something different the day you were arrested. The many things that you can imagine are amazing and endless. However, none of them will ever really satisfy your search.

If you are like I was, the reason for your unrest was based on the fact that you know that you had been doing too many wrong things that could have gotten you arrested before now. There are so many other crimes that could have brought you to prison that it is better not to think about them all. For me, the answer to my questions came as I realized that I could have come to prison for so many crimes. During the past 10 years, I had committed so many crimes that it was ridiculous just to blame one person for my incarceration.

Finally, I came to realize that I was the only person responsible for my troubles. Yes, nobody forced me to do any of the crimes I committed, not even the devil. I did it all because I held wrong beliefs and that led me to wrong actions. One of the examples of my wrong thinking while I was free as a young man was that I would not for anybody for a "stinking minimum salary" I wanted to be my own boss and do what I wanted. Yes, sound familiar? Well, that sounds tough, but it was just pure rebellion.

One of the examples of my wrong thinking while I was free as a young man was that I would not work for anybody or depend on them for their favor and payroll. I wanted to be a millionaire, yes, just like in the movies. See, to myself I was a man with a plan. But it was a plan that never worked.

That which I feared the most came to me. Ironically in prison I found myself working for.22 cents per hour, then.44 cents, and when they finally gave me .99 cents per hour in the prison industry, I thought I really had it going!!

The truth is that what happened to me was nothing else but the result of my wrong thinking. Had I held a different set of beliefs and ideas, I would have acted differently. Now, in prison, my mind was being forcibly transformed by this new reality. I knew it was time to begin changing my ideas if I was to survive this crisis.

My thinking began to change first, and then my emotions began to change. In other words, as my belief system changed, then the way I reacted to my environment changed.

You may think that it is all over and that you just have to sit tight, and the pain will go away. Please, allow me to say that the painful memories will never go away. But you can make some determinations that will change your present and future. There are no prison walls that the Power of God cannot overcome and there is no crime so bad that the Blood of Jesus can't forgive!!

I remember a word of wisdom that the Lord gave a man doing life in prison, which declared: That as the kings of the earth keep their valuable jewels "locked down" so the King of heaven is keeping some of His most precious jewels in lock down just for a season!!

"From heaven did the Lord behold the earth; to hear the groaning of the prisoner; to lose those that are appointed to death....."

(Ps. 102:19-20)

Chapter Three

How did I found God, Or rather, how He found me?

When I say that God has the answers that you need, and the answers the world needs to resolve the crime problem, I speak based on what God Himself has said. The Bible says that "unless you are born again" you will not change and you are without hope in this world, and in the world to come. (John 3) The Good News is that with God, all things are possible (Mark 9:23) and you can turn your life around. I am living proof of this fact!

During the first few months following my incarceration, I began to hear other inmates testifying about the Power of God to save and to heal. I was not interested in hearing that, but I was interested in getting out of the 23 hours of lock-down I was in!! Incidentally, the only guys that were allowed to go out to the yard to have service were the Christians. So, trying to be smart, I called their inmate pastor and told him to write my name on the list.

The next day, the time for the service came at 6:00 am. Great!! I was out of the cell and into the yard. Well, I found myself listening to the message "God saves and heals." I was not big on getting saved, since I did not know that I was lost, but I knew I needed healing for my soul.

After 3 months of listening to the GOOD NEWS from God, I realized that if I was going to survive, I had to make some changes. The first thing I had to do, if I wanted things to change, was to search for the God of the Bible that could empower me to change.

I was 29 years old and had not been able to control my life. I decided to give God a chance and convinced myself that He actually existed through reading His Word (Heb 11:6)

I did not want to read a book that proved His existence, but a book that took His existence for granted.

In the Bible, In the first chapter, in the first verse, it said, “In the beginning God....” I don’t think the existence of God needed to be proved. All the physical world proves that there is a designer behind every design. If you are breathing, eating, and existing, it is because there is something greater than that brought this about! So, I decided to learn how God worked with the Israelites, the non-Jews, and His church. I read how God dealt with individuals, nations, and the world in general. But what caught my attention in the Bible is a declaration that said, “the natural man receives not the things of the Spirit of God: for they are foolishness unto him, neither can he know them.” (I Cor. 2:14)

In other words, even if I attempted to read the Bible, I could not have understood the message, except beyond the simple command to repent. So, I realized that I needed to become spiritual in order to learn its many secrets.

CHAPTER FOUR

WHAT DOES IT MEAN TO BE BORN AGAIN?

The Bible declares in the Book of Romans, Chapter 3:23 that we "all have sinned, and come short of the glory of God". In another verse it says that the wages of sin is death, but the gift of God is eternal life" (Romans 6:23). These verses tell us that at one point there was a separation from God creating the need to go back to Him. The "going back to God" experience is termed in the Bible as "being born of the Spirit".

In searching the Bible, I found the same implication found in I Cor. 5: 17, which declares that "if any man is in Christ, he is a new creation...." Through these and other scriptures, I came to realize that I needed to be in Christ to be able to understand the ways and the mind of God. Then, I took my first step in what was going to be the most exciting journey of my life. I received the Lord Jesus into my heart according to the scriptures.

The Bible declared in Romans 10:9,10 that if I confess with my mouth that Jesus Christ is Lord and believe in my heart that God raised Him from the dead, I will be saved. Wow!!!

Yes, that was my first step in escaping from prison without leaving my cell. According to the Bible Jesus came "To open the blind eyes and to bring the prisoners out of prison, and them that sit in darkness out of the prison house."

(Isaiah 42:7)

The Bible declares that the people that sat in the region and shadow of death, light has sprung up" (Matthew 4:16). That was the place I was when God found me. And it may be the place you are now. At the new birth, we are translated from the kingdom of darkness into the kingdom of Jesus, and that we have passed from being a prisoner into the freedom of the Spirit.

I realized that if I was to play by God's rules, then I had to follow his instructions. If I wanted the results that God promised in the Bible, then I had to obey what the Bible told me about accepting His Son Jesus. I remember a definition of insanity that really stuck in my brain. An insane person is someone who always does the same thing and expects different results. Ha!!! Do you get that?

Now, when I received the Lord in my life it was only the beginning of a long journey. I knew that I had to do a lot of time in prison. That without some help I would probably end up dead or would add some more years to my already long sentence. I did not want to end up like the young man I had a conversation with early in my prison term.

This young man went to a juvenile center when he was 16 years old and was expected to be released at age 21. He was moved to the state facility when he was 18 years old to his sentence. There, he joined the local gang and they "assigned" him to murder an enemy. Acting under gang pressure and self-pride he went on and killed the person. At the time of our conversation, he was serving 3 life sentences, running consecutively. What a shame that young man will never be free again.

Once I found myself committed to the lordship of Jesus, I decided to avoid such pitfalls of the devil and instead learn the ways of God. I began to visit church services and read my Bible on a regular basis. I was a baby Christian when the enemy threw trouble against me. I ended up in segregation for a period of three months. Those of you who have been in isolation know how long the hours can become.

However, that time God used to teach me a lot of things. First, I received peace in my heart, and I began to read the Bible for hours.... I mean 10-15 hours a day. I read all night long because it was quiet, then I slept during the day's hours. I saved the food given to me during the day and consumed it during the night hours. After the last meal, I took my shower and then began to read. I stopped and ate something and read some more. I made instant coffee (see while you are under investigation the prison allowed you to purchase some items in the prison commissary. I continue that routine for many months until I finished reading the whole Bible. Praise God, I was often awake until 3:00 am when the guards came to do, they routinely count they were puzzled.

The Bible speaks that we should desire the milk of the Word to grow. So, that is what I did. Yes, I drank milk day and night. It is amazing to see how many brothers come to the Lord one day and the next day they think they are teachers or preachers of some kind. In my experience those brothers don't last long.

Once you come to God you must learn to be humble and meek to imitate us Father in all things. We have so many people bringing reproach to the Lord Jesus, by claiming to be Christians and acting like devils. Yes, that happens in the street as we as in prison. IN the street we were leaders, always giving orders and having people tell us how great we were. But now, in God things are different. If you want to be first, you must learn to be last.
"You shall seek me and find me when you shall search for me with all your heart."

CHAPTER FIVE

My personal encounter with the Lord

I knew that when we make Jesus the Christ Lord, His Holy Spirit comes to dwell in our hearts. I also believe that as we grow in the knowledge of Jesus, He will reveal himself to us in a greater measure. Our position of righteousness and our standing as sons of God we have from the moment we are born again, but the level of intimacy will increase as we draw near to Him.

The Bible declares that when the Holy Spirit baptizes a person into the body of Christ, he or she is a new creation (I Cor. 12:13) After that experience God considers the person righteous, a saint. Yes, the Apostle Paul called the members of the different churches saints when he was addressing the letters to the churches.

This fact, however, does not mean that we won't commit mistakes or never fall into diverse temptations. For in I John 1:9 and O John 2:1, the Bible tells people about the way to be free from their sins. Clearly, we won't need a lawyer or advocate if we have no sins. Jesus is our advocate with the Father.

In prison, you will see people that take their relationship with God very seriously. Others, however, seem as if their experience with God is something that has no bearing on their daily activities. I remember when the Lord Jesus entered my heart at the New Birth experience. Following the new birth experience, I grew hungry for His Word and His Presence. I read nothing but the Bible. As a result of my intimacy with His Word, I had a greater closeness with Jesus. In September of 1984, I had a special visitation from the Spirit of the Lord. It was during the afternoon hours when I was praying and groaning in my spirit. There the Lord answered my prayer. by visiting my cell (#27) at the state pen, and the Glory of God embraced me.

His presence was a tangible presence. I had been a drug user most of my adolescent years, but I had never experienced such a high. See, most of the time we used drugs to find comfort and harmony ourselves. When Jesus came into my cell, I had no words to communicate. I finally uttered a vow. I asked the Lord to lead me get out of prison alive and I would serve Him for the rest of my life.

I will never forget the words I heard in my spirit, **"You will see the goodness of God, in the land of the living…"** Jesus brought peace and harmony into my life at my lowest point. He is the Prince of Peace. That day He embraced me and comforted my soul like nothing else could ever do. I had cried to the Lord in such a state of desperation that what followed was nothing but a miracle.

The Lord promised to show Himself to those who love Him and obey Him. Those experiences are engraved in my heart so that I may not depart from my calling can have the same intimacy with Him right there in your cell. When we ask Him to come into your heart, He moves in along with all the love of the Father God for you. No, there is nothing special about me. God loves you even the same way He loves Jesus. Now I know that sometimes it is difficult for us to understand our right standing before God the Father. But that does not change the way God feels about us.

Sometimes we fail to realize that God in His Word has declared that He will remember our sins no more and that He has changed our hearts for good. In prison, all the conditions speak to you concerning your past and your terrible present. God has a different opinion of you. He sees you with no past, and with a bright future.

The Bible declares that God has great thoughts about us. It states that, "For I know the thoughts that I think about you, says the Lord, thoughts of peace and not of evil to give you an expected end." (Jeremiah 29:11) Yes, my fellow brother/ sister, you need to understand the cleansing effect that the eternal life of God produces in our hearts. We can't be playing church or faking that we are when you seek Him with something that we are not. Jesus is real and His Power will work on our behalf. You will find Him, all your heart.

CHAPTER SIX

It was on October 6, 1989 at the Federal Correctional Institution, Butner, NC, when I first heard teaching on the baptism of the Holy Spirit. Though I had read about it, I had never been taught on it. I did not know that there was, even more, to receive from God. In the past, I had heard people saying that "tongues" were of the devil, but I never remember speaking in other tongues before or during a drug deal. I had shot some people in the past, but never did I speak in unknown tongues as I was doing it! "Let every man be a liar, and God be true! (Romans 3:4)

So, the Full Gospel Businessmen's Fellowship group led me into this new baptism experience, which I gladly received. It was 9:45 am when I received the Baptism of the fire of the Holy Spirit in my life. I have never been the same.

When I received the baptism in the Holy Spirit a new language burst out from my spirit. This new language was so beautiful that I felt I was talking to God's face to face. I took hold of that language and have used it every day of my life since October 6, 1989.

Praise God for this wonderful experience with His Spirit. Now more than ever, God was embracing me with His presence. God was visiting my spirit d soul, making it His dwelling place. The new language was not an exception in God's mind, but an essential element to my spiritual growth and relationship with Him.

As I stated before, I know that there are some brothers who will argue against this experience, but they have no scriptural ground, their opposition is based on traditional beliefs, not Bible facts. What the early church received as a gift for their lives, we may also receive, for God is no respected of persons.

If they needed the baptism of the Holy Spirit in the 1st century, we surely need it in the 21st century. There is much more that we could say about this great experience, but that is not the purpose at this time. One thing I know, if you don't believe in speaking with new tongues as the Bible teaches, don't worry.... you won't. For a gift to be a gift, it is necessary to have a willing recipient. Just know that God Himself promised He would give the baptism in the Holy Spirit to those who ask Him in faith (Luke 11:9-13) This wonderful experience gave me the strength and the power I needed to live the Christian life I was commanded to live for Jesus. I knew that I loved Jesus with all my heart for many years, but when the Holy Spirit came into my life, I experienced a new level of love and appreciation for the God who died for me. I could feel every tear He shed for me. I could vividly see Jesus hanging on the cross, looking into the future at me, the prisoner of sin and death that He was dying to save.

LET GOD FIND YOU

The Bible said, that "if we confess with our mouth the Lord Jesus and believe in our heart that God has raised Him from the dead, we shall be saved". If you believe in your heart that Jesus died for your sins, and you are ready to begin a new life, pray this prayer out loud:

Lord God, I come to you in the Name of you Son Jesus. I repent from being a sinner, and for all the wrongdoing. I believe that Jesus is your Son and the Savior of the world. I believe that you raised Him from the dead and now He is reigning with you. I ask you Jesus to come into my heart and make me a new creature according to the scriptures. I ask you Lord to give me the grace to serve this prison time and to be the best Christian I can be.

I ask you Lord God to be my Father, and to provide a way out of every temptation that I may face during this time. I will always give you the glory and the praises that you deserve, in Jesus' name I pray. Amen.

In walking with God there have to be total cooperation for His guidance and direction. We should not rest on what we see but on the new ideas we get from the Word of God. For me the key word is changing the way I used to do things.

CHAPTER SEVEN

Now that I am a Christian, what's Next?

I decided to do part two of this instructional book in order to introduce some significant teaching material. However, I could not have done this without introducing you first to the Lord. The Bible declares that the natural man does not receive either understand the things of God. But now, you are no more a natural man if you have made Jesus the Lord of your life.

What follows in Part Two is dedicated to those of you who have decided to give God a chance to change your life. There are two ways to do prison time, with or without God. I have seen people doing a lot of years in prison without God. Their mental deterioration and Deprivation have been notable. Some others have lived all their prison time thinking about revenge and going back to their old ways. What a waste of time. On the other hand, those who have done their time trusting in God and using all the opportunities to improve themselves have come out in victory! The Christian life is a life of freedom and joy, for the Lord is the source of our strength and power. He who waits on the Lord shall renew his strength daily.

So, let us examine one opportunity, the opportunity to educate ourselves. Whether your institution provides education or not, you can always find ways to study and improve yourself.

EDUCATION IS FOR YOU!!!

In most places the prison system provides some minimum education programs such as GED. I realize that some places are so crowded that it may take up to a year to start on a program, but you have the time, and it is better late than never.

When I came to prison, I had been a high school dropout for years. My last contact with the education system had been in 1974 when I took the GED test. When Jesus came into my life, I knew that received the life of God in me. I knew that I could do all things through Him. Yes, that included schooling. So, I enrolled in a four-year college program, finishing (3.2 GPA) with a bachelor's degree in business administration. I also took a paralegal course, which helps me immensely, as well as many other courses. In those days the education programs were better, for the whole system was into rehabilitation. Today, the system is punishment-oriented.

Nonetheless, there are still some programs available. Don't fight against education! Take advantage of these programs. They will help you not only survive but succeed in the street, and even in prison. I took a paralegal course and used the knowledge to take my case back to court. (Yes, I won!!!)

I realized that the changes God was producing in me were permanent and that upon my release, I would have to live a life that was drug-free and crime-free. I knew that I was not stupid, as the devil had always told me. But I was smart as Jesus said we could be. All the devil can do is lie and deceive us. Gut Jesus came that we may have life and have it more abundantly. The life of God is in me now. So how can I be stupid if God is in me? Now I am finishing my Master degree in divinity, and maybe later, a doctorate. Ha!!!! Yes, with God in me I can do all things.

At this point, I would like to bring to your attention the idea that even though with God all things are possible, all things are not necessarily probable. The main player in this equation is us, you and me. If we do what the Word said to do, the thing will come to pass as the Lord promised, but if we just quote the Word and keep acting crazy, nothing will change.

See, faith is believing God at His Word, but that faith without corresponding action is dead, idle, and will bring no fruit. In the Bible only those who submitted to the will of God obtained the promises of God. And every time they got out of the will of God a lot of bad things happened to them.

<u>NOW THAT YOU ARE SAVED....FIGHTING OLD HABITS</u>

Just because you are incarcerated does not mean that you have to act like some kind of caveman. Some people think that because they are in prison that gives them the right to abuse other fellow men or to act like some Cro-Magnon from the Stone Age. It is so ridiculous when I see guys that have been in prison for a few weeks or months, and they see a woman on TV. They act like a pervert.

Hey, keep your class brother; you just got here I used to say.

We need to understand that habits are vicious forces that we acquired during our years of sin. Don't be surprised if you find that you revert to the habits of anger, fear, and depression. You just have to remember that Jesus has set you free, and "He who the Son sets free is free indeed."

You can dominate all habits (Phil. 4:13) Just don't give room to the devil with feelings of condemnation and guilt. Stand up in your position as a child of God and speak out to the demons and the powers of darkness that you will not sin against God. Confess that you are strong in the power of His might.

When you are tempted to use the name of the Lord in vain, remember that it is a sin in which the Lord will not take you as innocent. Then, face the fact that you did it, confess your sin, and confess that He is just and righteous to forgive you.

Pray, "*<u>Father, I ask you to clean my lips and remove this habit from my mind and mouth. Fil my mouth with praises to my Lord.</u>* Amen"

You will see how God will honor that prayer. In your walk with Lord in prison you will learn that when we become a Christian, we must learn to place old habits and our flesh under submission. We need to respect our wives in the visiting room and even other women in that place. Walking in holiness is one of these things we must learn from the Word.

However, a misconception of God's commandment to be holy may cause you unnecessary pain. Living holy in prison does not mean that you don't feel anything, or that you will never have a desire to be with a woman. To be holy means to be separated for God's purpose.

To be holy or walk-in holiness means that you will not submit to be body-ruled, but that you will trust in God to give you the strength to do what is pleasing before God. God will not call you to do something impossible to achieve. His yoke is easy, and His burden is light.

Many religious people have brought a bad connotation to God and his commandments. They have associated ministry with misery, and holiness with bitterness. See, God wants us to be holy because He is Holy. He is not going to call us to do something He is not doing Himself, or something we can't do.

The call to walk in holiness is a call to be separated for God's purpose. It is a call to be distinguished from this world because of our relationship with God. The meaning of the word holy is separation. During the Old Testament times, separation from God was accomplished in many areas. They separated, people, places, and things.

Once these things were separated, the only legal use was for that purpose and intention for which it was separated, and that was to honor God's use, or holiness, which is done by the Spirit of God. God is calling His people to be separated for his use. For in a great house, there are not only vessels of gold and silver, but also of wood and clay: some to honor and some to dishonor. When the Apostle Paul wrote these words to Timothy, he had all Christians in his mind. For the principle established here still prevails in our days. Here the Spirit is not talking about our worth before God, but of our usability. God wants to use us to evangelize the world. He has a great desire that no one will perish, but that all come to the saving knowledge of Jesus. God in this saving endeavor needs us to accomplish that purpose.

Those who become Christians in prison are no different from those who find salvation in the free world. We have the same spirit, the same faith, and the same grace that saves us all. In actuality, I have seen greater manifestations of the Spirit of God in prison than in most churches outside.

I have seen prisoners delivered from cigarette addiction. I have seen homosexuals changed by the power of God into men on honor. I have experienced the evidence of healing by the laying on of hands and by the prayer of the elders, just as the Bible declares, right in the middle of the prison walls.

I want to encourage you to put into practice what we have talked about her, and to make a quality decision to walk in a manner worthy of the Lord. In other words, live what you believe. The Bible says that we are born of God and therefore, sons of God. Well, this statement implies that we should be imitators of God our Father (Ephesians 5:1).

Therefore, every Sunday (whether you feel like it or not) put on your ironed clothes and go to the chapel to worship. There you can sing hymns and sometimes give testimonies about what God has done for you.

We are an open letter read by all inmates, and you know that we like to read in between the lines. If we say that we are of God but act like a devil, we are deceiving ourselves, and we bring reproach to the name of the Lord. All other religions are saying that what we have is not real, but the fact is they cannot prove it. Truly, Jesus has the power to change the most unlikely candidate into a man of God. He did it with me and He will do it with you, if you will submit yourself to God and resist the devil (not the other way around)

CHAPTER EIGHT

I will not be defeated; I will never fail

The only way to stay in victory is to be transformed by the renewing of your mind. In other words, change your mindset. You must make a conscious decision concerning the things of God. That is to make a conscious decision to adhere to the Bible instruction for your new life in Christ.

I have listed several spiritual exercise and practices which I did for as long as I was in prison. Well, one thing that I put to the test is the fact that the Word of God tells us to be continually filled with the Spirit. This commandment implies that there are going to be times when the "spiritual tank" will not be full to the top. Let the words of Christ dwell in you richly in all wisdom: teaching and admonishing one another in psalms and hymns and spiritual songs, singing with grace to the Lord." (Col 3:16)

Now, there are some Christian disciplines that we must master in order to keep ourselves full of the Spirit and power. We must learn to walk in love, to stay in communion with the Spirit of God and You will never fail, for love never fails.

The FIRST exercise is the Exercise of Prayer.

In Christianity there are many great definitions of prayer. Some of them follow the traditional understanding that prayer is a means of communication and communion with God. I, however, would like to bring my definition of prayer along this line: Prayer is our God-given way of communicating by which we exercise our authority to put into motion spiritual laws that will bring into our reality whatsoever God has determined in His Word that we may receive.

Furthermore, in prayer and through prayer we move ourselves to know the mind and purposes of God toward the world and us. Prayer is a discipline that will accompany us as long as we dwell in our earthly tabernacle, for God has decreed to act in response to our prayers and supplications, and not beyond that. It is important that we understand this statement in relation to the restored authority that Jesus has given to mankind in his name and in the power of His Holy Spirit.

The second exercise is the study of the Word of God, the Bible. Since the Word is a supernatural book from a supernatural God it will accomplish tremendous work in our lives.

However, there has to be a special effort on our part to sit down every day and allow the Spirit to teach us what is the mind of God as it is found in the Word. We need to realize that God has not said all He is ever going to say, but He has declared unto us the things that we need to know to have a successful life. For the secret things belong to the Lord, but what we understand He has revealed to us. We must understand that there is no substitute for the reading of the Word.

There are many good writers and thousands of good books on a variety of subjects. But they are digested food from somebody else. The most nutritious meal you will ever have is the one you digest yourself. Let the entrance of the Word of God create light in your spirit as the Father intended it. God knows best.

The third exercise is meditation in the Word of God, the Bible.

After we have read the Word, we must stay in a fixed position and ponder the Word. Meditation is defined as "stead gazing" or as continually considering a specific thing. The purpose of meditation is to bring out the best of the new creation. This new creation has been imparted with the resources, wisdom, and might for life and godliness. There is no need for us to attempt to improve what God has already done by effectively renewing our spirit. Where we really need help is in the realm of the mind. The mind needs to be transformed by the renewing of our old thought patterns.

God has done a marvelous job in our spirits at the new birth. But we need to bring out the fruit that God has placed in our inner man through the Holy Spirit. In the book of Joshua, God told Joshua "This book of the law shall not depart out of your mouth, but thou shall meditate therein day and night...." What was the purpose of this commandment from God? Was it to just Joshua? No!!! The purpose of this commandment of this order from God was the Joshua would be prosperous in all the things God had planned for his life and the life of his people.

The fourth exercise is the discipline of praise and worship.

Our spirit, mind, and body will be submitted to God as we learn to yield ourselves to praise the Lord every day no matter what the circumstances may look like. I had the practice of praising the Lord early in the morning. I realize that the morning hours are not the best time when are locked down. You must create a habit of doing it. I composed more than 100 songs during incarceration. These songs may not make a dollar in the commercial world, but I know that they pleased my Father. I could always feel the presence of God as I worship His Holy name.

Finally, we must consider the works that we must do in correspondence to our beliefs. Jesus said, "If any man serves me, him my Father will honor" (John 12:26) Serving Jesus is simply doing what He said in His Word. Jesus chastised those folks in his time for being only hearers of the Word and not doers. Later, in the book of James, he emphasized the need to bring the corresponding action to the faith that we have. Our faith is our conviction based on what we heard about God. Faith, or our beliefs, is the foundation of our hope, and therefore, what keeps us going. In prison, we have declared that we are born of God and therefore, sons of God. Well, this statement implies that we should be imitators of God our Father.

I want to encourage you to put into practice what we have talked about here and to make a quality decision for the Lord. You will prove your enemies to be wrong. And you will taste and eat the good of the land. Prison time is not wasted time if you find your destiny in God. And the God of peace will guard your heart, mind, and body until the day that we will see the face of our precious Redeemer. It will be there that I will say thank you Lord for loving me with an everlasting love.

"FOR GOD SO LOVED THE WORLD, THAT HE GAVE HIS ONLY BEGOTTEN SON THAT WHOSOEVER BELIEVED IN HIM SHALL SHAL NOT PERISH"

...JOHN 3:16

www.ingramcontent.com/pod-product-compliance
Lightning Source LLC
LaVergne TN
LVHW070155110826
845147LV00002B/409

* 9 7 8 1 7 3 6 7 8 4 3 2 7 *